THE PINK ELEPHANT

A BREAST CANCER SURVIVOR'S
JOURNEY,
SELF-DISCOVERY AND
LIFE LESSONS

LATHA SRINIVASAN

notionpress.com

INDIA • SINGAPORE • MALAYSIA

ISBN 979-8-89133-624-7

For my dearest Amma.

This book, my achievements, and life as I know it, would not be possible without Amma's immense love, unwavering support and unshakeable belief that I can conquer the world.

Her blessings remain eternal.

CONTENTS

AUTHOR'S NOTE

When I was studying in college in Chennai, Tamil Nadu, I never knew what my life would turn out like over the next decade. I believed that like most girls from my community, I would have an arranged marriage by the time I was 25 or 26 and end up being a homemaker looking after the kids. But in the next few years, the curveball that came hurtling towards me was extremely fast, unexpected and changed my destiny.

I was diagnosed with breast cancer (Stage 2) in April 2004 and that year turned out to be the most difficult, painful and traumatic one in my happy-go-lucky life. The shocking emotional upheaval that followed was something I had not anticipated. The sun disappeared and the days that followed the diagnosis were dark, gloomy and depressing.

Padma Vibhushan Awardee, Ramon Magsaysay Awardee and former Chairperson of The Cancer Institute (Chennai), Dr. V Shanta, was my oncologist and the inspiration she provided me (and thousands of cancer patients) was invaluable. She taught me to sail through my treatment (chemotherapy, radiation, surgery and hormonal therapy) and recovery with hope, and value life.

Breast cancer is one of the most common cancers in India and today, there have been significant strides in new medicines, therapies and treatment methods. Survival rates for breast cancer in India stand at 66% while in the United States it is an astounding 90% to 95%. Sadly, in India, survival rates are low due to lack of awareness and late diagnosis, among other factors.

The symbol for breast cancer is a pink ribbon and cancer is the elephant in the room. Ergo. The Pink Elephant. The Pink Elephant is not just a pick-me-up for women diagnosed with breast cancer – I believe these words will also resonate with caregivers and with those in the medical profession. In fact, this book is for one and all as it seeks to spread breast cancer awareness and help improve a person's quality of life.

This is my first book and I have always wanted to write about the lessons I learnt during my treatment and recovery. Many of friends kept telling me I was an inspiration to them and I realized that the Big C is a disease most people are terrified of. I have seen other women diagnosed with breast cancer go through severe emotional distress and it struck me that I needed to share my transformative experience with all to help patients heal more effectively and caregivers provide ample support. In India, counselling for cancer patients and their families is still not as common as it should be in hospitals. In fact, I have counselled numerous patients over the years when I have gone in for my regular check-ups.

Cancer is a disease that not only impacts and changes the life of a patient but also their families. Neither the patient nor their families can predict how the treatment and recovery process will affect their lives – individually and as a unit.

As proved by various studies, breast cancer patients undergo psychosocial problems and as a patient, a patient's family and caregiver, it is important to understand them. Loss, fear, anger, depression, anxiety, uncertainty, low self-esteem and impairment of body image are common emotions and issues a patient undergoes. And I underwent them as well.

My transformative experience was through understanding my emotional journey and self-discovery. Thus, I have deliberately divided the chapters into emotions rather than follow a chronological timeline or dissect the treatment. Wisdom doesn't come through or with a timeline but with experiences, isn't it?

Talking and writing about my cancer experience is part of my healing process and today, I have a renewed zest for life. My breast cancer journey also led me to self-discovery and I would like to share that story to nudge you towards your path to self-discovery.

As you start reading The Pink Elephant, my final word is this - don't ignore symptoms of any kind – see a doctor ASAP; get a yearly health check-up once you hit 40 (including a mammogram for women); and if you are a cancer patient, do your cancer follow-ups diligently. As oncologists tell you, breast cancer can be cured if detected early.

All women and men, young and old, will hopefully learn how to lead more fulfilling, enriching and joyous lives – as I have – as they go through these pages.

Latha Srinivasan

1

FEAR

Fear. Fear is an emotion that everyone experiences and has experienced at some point in their lives. But the fear of life and death is something most people do not go through when they are in their 30s and 40s. Contemplating one's demise at that age is inconceivable but I learnt there are circumstances in life that can lead us to that.

I clearly remember the day I first found out about the tumour in my left breast. It was a bright sunny day in Chennai in March 2004. I went to a GP in Mylapore (Chennai) and told her about the slight blood discharge from my left breast and she examined me. As soon as she completed the examination, she told me to get a mammogram done immediately. I rushed to the diagnostic centre in Nandanam (Chennai) with my mother in tow and waited anxiously for the results. My mother was calm, as always.

The first emotion that I felt when the doctor examined my left breast and asked me to do a mammogram was fear. Was it a tumour? Was it cancer? When I got the mammogram results and headed back to my doctor, the news was devastating. Yes, it was a tumour and she was sure it was cancerous. I broke down. There was no holding back the flood of tears and along with it came the crushing fear. The fear of death. Would I survive? Would I die? Was it just breast cancer? Had the cancer spread to other parts of my body? How long did I have to live?

I started to feel myriad emotions and a thousand thoughts bombarded my mind at the same time. I had no control over my emotions or thoughts and the overwhelming fear that gripped me is what I remember to this day. How does one ever forget that moment? This was a live or die situation and when the fear of death hits you so unexpectedly, you feel like it's the end - the end of your life as you knew it. When the first diagnosis is given, there is so much uncertainty attached to everything right from the type of treatment, your body's response to the treatment, and the life changes that accompany it all. And yes, survival itself.

For most people though, the first question that hits them when they hear the diagnosis is - Why me? Why me? Why me? This is often followed by other questions like — am I not a good person? What did I do to deserve this? Does God not love me? What wrongs have I committed for such a punishment? What I learnt in my journey through breast cancer is that it is ALRIGHT to experience and express your fears. The only thing we need to learn is how to deal with this fear.

Fear is a natural emotional response when one is going through a major crisis in life. A traumatic incident automatically triggers a variety of emotions, including fear, and the uncertainty of life you feel when you receive the news that you have cancer can be overwhelming. So, it is OK to experience fear - but you need to learn how to manage it, overcome it and how to move forward successfully for your own mental and physical well-being.

In order to overcome fear, you first need to accept your cancer diagnosis. Don't be in denial. Turn to family and friends and talk about your fears. Write down your fears and analyse the positives. If required, seek counselling.

Positive thinking is crucial, especially in the treatment of cancer, and from fear you need to move to positivity. Start planning the next steps you need for your treatment – or even any life situation you may be facing. Most important, understand that fear is temporary and this emotion will pass. Fear can be conquered.

My mantra for combatting fear:

1. Acknowledge it.

2. Accept it.

3. Experience it.

4. Analyse it.

5. Move forward.

6. Be positive.

7. Seek emotional support.

8. Seek therapy.

2

ANXIETY AND STRESS

Anxiety and stress. Anxiety and stress creeps up on us in many situations and the level of anxiety differs in every instance. Will we pass that exam? Will we get a good performance review? Will we make the flight on time? The list is endless. But the level of stress and anxiety one feels when one is given a medical diagnosis like breast cancer is like none other.

Anxiety and stress disorders get triggered due to excessive fear and worry, and when undergoing breast cancer treatment, many women are prone to them. Studies have confirmed this as well. Stress and anxiety are common among breast cancer patients but their levels keep varying during the course of treatment. They are always lurking at the back of your mind ready to jump at you at the drop of a hat.

I experienced anxiety and stress on many days of the treatment process – when I went in for medical tests, doctor's appointments, the surgery and even during the recovery process. How was my treatment going? How was body my responding to the drugs and radiation? Will I recover completely in six months? What update would the oncologist share every time?

Anxiety and stress can affect your mental health and, most importantly, your recovery process. Numerous studies ((1) and (2)) have also proved this. You also tend to feel physical symptoms, like loss of appetite, nausea, vomiting, insomnia and panic attacks.

I felt most of these symptoms too, not just because of chemotherapy, but due to anxiety and stress. So how did I deal with this? I turned to my friends and family who were more than happy to support me. They ensured that I didn't feel lonely and included me in all their activities. Often, I would head off for sleepovers at my friends' homes, step out for movies, chill out in cafes and go shopping.

Filling my life with various activities during treatment gave me less time to brood and mope over my health, and more time to enjoy the good things and improve my quality of life. This was a big factor in helping me get through treatment and boosting my mental health.

Another factor that can help bring down stress and anxiety is getting a pet. Of course, this is a personal choice but the unconditional love, support and companionship of pets has the power to help us in the healing process. When humans engage and cuddle with pets, the levels of dopamine (neurotransmitter related to movement, feeling pleasure), serotonin (neurotransmitter related to digestion and metabolism) and oxytocin (the 'love' hormone) increase. This reduces stress levels, makes us feel good and sleep better. Today, animal therapy has been widely embraced in the West to treat mental health.

I have always been a pet lover and had a dog right from my college days. It was ironic though that my adorable pet Dachshund, Brownie, passed away in December 2003, just a few months before my cancer diagnosis. I had moved to Bengaluru from Chennai in November 2003 for work and I didn't have the heart to get a new pet immediately. Brownie had been my most lovable and trusted companion through my other low phases in life and yet, when I needed her the most, she wasn't around. I often wondered whether she passed away before my diagnosis because she wouldn't be able to handle seeing me ill. Post Brownie, Zen, a Cocker Spaniel, came into my life for a decade and gave me so much joy. Now, it is my Beagle, Yuki, who is the center of my world and who brightens each day.

My mantra to deal with stress and anxiety:

1. Think positive.

2. Get a pet.

3. Engage in activities.

4. Practice yoga.

5. Practice Pranayama.

6. Meditate.

7. Go for walks.

8. Seek emotional support.

9. Seek therapy.

References

(1) Wang X, Wang N, Zhong L, et al. Prognostic value of depression and anxiety on breast cancer recurrence and mortality: a systematic review and meta-analysis of 282,203 patients. Mol Psychiatry. 2020;25(12):3186-3197. doi:10.1038/s41380-020-00865-6

(2) Moreno-Smith M, Lutgendorf SK, Sood AK. Impact of stress on cancer metastasis. Future Oncology 2010; 6(12):1863–1881.

3

DEPRESSION

Depression. Who hasn't experienced sadness? Everyone has. Who has experienced depression? Perhaps some of us. Studies have shown that depression hits about 30% to 50% of breast cancer patients (1). Emotional distress is common among cancer patients and as time goes on, sadness can turn into depression for some. The fear, uncertainty and body changes one experiences can get overwhelming and this is when patients need complete support and understanding.

I never went into depression post my diagnosis probably because I was immediately cushioned by my family and friends who ensured that I was kept engaged as far as possible. But not every woman's situation is the same. You could be a breast cancer patient who is living with her parents, or has young children, or be elderly. There is no 'one size fits all' solution to preventing and treating depression during this time. But we can use tried and tested methods to overcome sadness and depression.

Now, how do you spot depression? You'll possibly feel (among other symptoms) constantly low, experience tremendous fear and anxiety, be unable to cope with daily tasks and have difficulty sleeping. One can also be subject to panic attacks. If you go through these symptoms for more than a few weeks, you must reach out to your GP or psychologist and get a proper diagnosis and treatment plan. Counselling and therapy are also some things you can consider to treat depression.

Remember that feeling depressed is normal when you undergo breast cancer diagnosis and treatment – this is NOTHING to be ashamed of. Talk about it and seek help. This will aid in the healing process and give you a better quality of life.

My mantra to help cope with depression:

1.   Keep a check on symptoms.

2.   Engage in activities.

3.   See a GP/ psychologist.

4.   Seek emotional support.

5.   Seek therapy.

References

(1) National Cancer Institute. Depression. https:// www.cancer.gov/about-cancer/coping/feelings/ depression-pdq, 2019.

4

ANGER AND RESENTMENT

Anger and resentment. Anger and resentment often tag along with the emotions of fear and anxiety post a breast cancer diagnosis, and you could continue to feel them even after recovery. There were days I felt angry and resentful towards the world because of what I was going through. I didn't deserve this. I had lost so much because of breast cancer. My life would never be normal again. Would I ever get married and have kids? Would my future be bright? Would I find joy in life again? These thoughts and questions can crop up over and over again and your anger and resentment can increase with time.

One fine day in June 2004, I decided that this anger and resentment was not worth it. Other than making me an emotional wreck, it was not helping me improve my situation in any form or manner. Could my anger and resentment make the breast cancer diagnosis disappear? NO. I had to go through the treatment and the sooner I learnt to accept this the better I would feel and heal. But not all women can take this pragmatic approach as easily as I did.

One of the best advices that psychologists give is to channel anger and resentment positively rather than negatively. In fact, this advice is applicable to any crisis in life. In this case, don't use the anger and resentment you feel to bog you down but use it to beat cancer.

My mantra to deal with anger and resentment:

1. Understand it.

2. Avoid the triggers.

3. Find new energy outlets.

4. Exercise.

5. Practice Yoga.

6. Engage in new activities.

7. Seek change.

8. Seek emotional support.

9. Seek therapy.

5

LOSS

Loss. Loss is an emotion people usually associate with someone's demise. But loss is a strong emotion you feel when you go through cancer as well. Unlike most diseases, cancer is all-consuming and wreaks physical and emotional havoc. With breast cancer, women have to deal with loss – loss of their breast/s, loss of their hair, loss of perceived femininity and sexuality.

When I started my breast cancer treatment in April 2004, Dr. Shanta had said I needed six rounds of chemotherapy (use of drugs to kill the cancer cells in the body) and a mastectomy (removal of the breast). My treatment started with several rounds of chemotherapy and radiation, followed by the mastectomy, which would again be followed by chemotherapy and radiation. I would also need to undergo an oophorectomy (removal of the ovaries) at some point in life to reduce chances of the cancer recurring.

The first time I underwent chemotherapy treatment, I didn't know what to expect. I was required to stay overnight at the hospital so that the oncologists could monitor my reaction to the strong, powerful chemicals. With Amma in tow as always, I got myself admitted at The Cancer Institute and waited. The room was stark with four empty walls, devoid of any technology and the only television in the ward was in the main waiting area. Amma and I watched TV for a while till the nurses and oncologist came to administer my first chemotherapy which would last several hours.

As I lay on that hospital bed in the somber room, the nurse quickly hooked up the IV (intravenous drip) and then proceeded to inject a large amount of dark red liquid into it. I could feel the saline mixed with medicine slowly coursing through my body and the process lasted over two hours. I had already been updated about the side effects of chemotherapy which typically include hair loss, nausea, vomiting, fatigue, weakness, loss of appetite, anemia, low immunity, infections, sore mouth, diarrhea or constipation, and insomnia. After the chemotherapy session, I was advised to take as much rest as possible and eat bland food and have plenty of liquids. I didn't sleep too well at the hospital because I just wanted to come home – to my familiar environs, to my room, to my bed, to my soft pillows.

I was told that the toughest period would be the first five days after chemotherapy when most of the symptoms hit you hard. As the strong drugs wear off after five or six days, you start to feel better but not normal of course. I remember breezing through the first chemotherapy with aplomb and was quite chuffed. I hardly felt the symptoms but was cautious and rested at home for a week. The focus was on following the oncologist's instructions to a T with regard to my diet and do's and don'ts.

However, the second round of chemo which I underwent after three weeks was another story. I had severe nausea and could not keep down any food. I was throwing up constantly and survived on a liquid diet, sleeping most of the time. My body was weak and I needed help even to go to the bathroom. But once the first week went by, I was able to step out and meet friends.

One day, I remember I was watching a movie with a friend at his place, when I ran my hand through my shoulder-length hair and out came a clump of hair. I panicked and told my friend, "Oh my god! My hair is falling out!" I didn't know what to do. Was I going to watch all my hair fall off like this? Was I going to have bald patches on my head? How do I deal with this?

As soon as I reached home, I called another friend and narrated what had happened. She asked to come over the next day and when I landed up, she quickly dragged me to her bathroom.

"Wait here and trust me," she told me.

When she came back in a few minutes, she was a holding a new razor in one hand and a chair in the other. She made me sit with my head in the sink and proceeded to shave off my hair! I didn't utter a word.

"Now look," she smiled pleased with her art work and turned me towards the mirror. There I was, no hair and perfectly bald round head. I touched my fuzzy head and both of us started giggling. I felt damn good. I didn't need to see my hair fall out in clumps over the next few months and get stressed every time – instead, I chose to take control of the situation and got my head shaved off.

I decided then that I would force myself to get back to normal life – eat out, watch movies and even go to parties. And through it all, I would take the necessary precautions. But I definitely wouldn't let cancer get the better of me.

The following week my friends took me to a party at a luxury hotel and the hosts were handing out awards to guests for best dressed and so on through the night. Lo and behold, I won the award for best hairstyle and I was just over the moon! No one knew I was undergoing cancer treatment - people thought I had gone to a temple and shaved my head due to a mannat (religious vow). From taking control of my hair loss situation, I found the courage to handle the chemo sessions that followed and felt ready to take things head on. Moreover, my hair was going to grow back, isn't it?

But the mastectomy surgery I had to undergo in September 2004 was one I was not prepared for. I had never undergone any surgery in life and this was a major one. Dr. Shanta was performing the surgery and while I had complete faith in her, I didn't know what it would be like or mean for me. And as per the treatment process at the time, a breast reconstruction could be done only after I completed five years in remission.

Now, for women, their hair and breasts represent their feminine identity and sexuality. A woman's body image is severely impacted when she experiences hair loss and the removal of a breast/s. This can trigger a whole range of emotions, especially loss and grief, and affect how a woman perceives herself. Right from the ancient times across cultures, a woman's hair and breasts represented her sexual attractiveness and was important to their self-worth. Long hair and breasts implied beauty, fertility and all that embodied the feminine. A woman's locks are part of her identity and in Indian culture, long hair is treasured. Even in Indian mythology and Hinduism, apsaras and goddesses are all blessed with long tresses and beautiful bosoms. Many Indian women who go through breast cancer are particularly worried about the social stigma of hair loss and feel ashamed of it. They feel less feminine and this mindset can be changed only with counselling and constant reassurance.

Undergoing the mastectomy (for me, it was the removal of the left breast) was not an issue for me because that was mandatory for my well-being. But how would I feel after that? How would I cope with the loss of a breast? Would I feel different? Would this affect my sexuality? Unlike my hair, which would grow back in a few months, I had to wait for years for a breast reconstruction surgery.

I was estrogen receptor positive (ER positive) and thus, was on hormone therapy for five years. This treatment blocks hormones (I didn't get my periods) and aids/ reduces chances of the cancer from recurring. Since I was just 32 and single, Dr. Shanta had told me that I could decide in the future as to when I wanted to have my ovaries removed (oophorectomy) in case I wanted to have children. So many aspects were changing for me as a woman.

It was around that time that an incident happened which changed my perspective on this whole issue. My friends and I were out for dinner a month or so after my surgery. A friend's friend, a doctor, was visiting from Delhi and he knew about my situation. As we got chatting, he looked at me and said, "Listen, you have been given a second chance."

"How???" I asked him.

"Now you can get the breast size that you really want when you do the reconstruction!" he smiled.

I started laughing.

That statement made me feel so good. In the West, many women get breast implants (or a boob job as it's known in common parlance) to get bigger breasts because they are unhappy with their breast size. This breast enhancement boosts their confidence levels. In my case, I was getting breast reconstruction as part of my cancer journey.

I am grateful to the visiting doctor for giving me a different perspective and teaching me that I am no less of a woman. In fact, I was all woman! At the end of the day, it is what you feel inside – you need to feel good and you need to feel feminine. When you are confident and feel like a woman, then the world will treat you exactly the way you want to be treated. I was as feminine as any woman and I was going to make sure no one saw me any differently. Love yourself and the world will love you.

My mantra for handling loss:

1. Love yourself.

2. Practice self-care.

3. Develop confidence.

4. Develop strength.

5. Find outlets.

6. Be active.

7. Seek support.

8. Seek emotional counseling.

Fertility

Breast cancer treatment can affect fertility and women, who want children after treatment, must discuss this with their oncologist. According to studies, chemotherapy can impact the ovaries which could result in infertility or difficulty in the ability to get pregnant. In the West, women undergoing breast cancer treatment often get their eggs frozen and in India, this option is available now.

Mastectomy and Breast Reconstruction

Today, there has been tremendous advancement in breast cancer treatment so when you have a mastectomy you can simultaneously have a breast reconstruction. Speak to your oncologist about the various options and the best option for you. Please note that this varies from patient to patient based on numerous factors, including the type and stage of cancer.

6

HOPE

Hope. What is life without hope? As humans, we thrive and survive on hope. Tomorrow will be a good day. I will feel better in a while. I'll do well in the next exam. Human tendency is to always perceive the worst when something – especially negative - happens in life. But hope played a major role in helping me through breast cancer and surviving it.

The single most important decision in my life in April 2004 was as to which oncologist I wanted to get treated under for breast cancer. A friend had suggested that I meet Dr. V Shanta and also go to a well-known chain of hospitals so I can figure out the treatment each offered and which oncologist I was most comfortable with.

I first went to meet the oncologist at the popular hospital chain and found the hospital quite spic-and span and stereotypical – pristine white walls, large well-furnished waiting rooms and corridors, sparkling glass windows and very few patients around. When I met the oncologist, I asked him about the course of treatment, the side effects and recovery time. He was very professional and I didn't find anything lacking in him or the hospital.

The next day I had an appointment at the Cancer Institute (Adyar, Chennai) with Dr. V Shanta. The Cancer Institute was in stark contrast to the hospital I had been to a day earlier – there were hundreds of people milling about. It was like a mela. Many were waiting to see the doctor, some were in line for radiation, some for billing, and yet others for medical tests. It was an endless sea of faces, young and old, that I saw across the hospital. Most of them seemed to be from the middle and lower middle class and it was later I learnt why – the Cancer Institute does a lot of free cancer treatment for those who cannot afford it.

The corridors here were neither pristine nor was there fancy furniture. But what I saw were dozens of smiling faces and people who were going about cancer treatment in a very matter-of-fact way and they seemed to be leading completely normal lives. It astounded me that no one here looked fearful or agitated and this gave me a surge of hope. Hope which I desperately needed.

The Cancer Institute oncologists see patients on a first come, first serve basis, and mom and I waited several hours to meet Dr. Shanta. When my name was finally called out, I was relieved but also really scared. All I wanted to know by then was – would I be OK? As soon as I walked into Dr. Shanta's room, I burst into tears. She patted me on the back gently and told me to sit down while she examined my medical reports. Though she and her assistant just took about five or six minutes to go through the reports, to me it seemed like years. Dr. Shanta then turned to me, smiled and said, "Don't worry, you will be fine."

Those words she uttered 19 years ago still ring in my ears and I remember them all the time. The hope that I felt when I walked into that hospital rose a thousand-fold when I met her and I knew I wanted her to be my oncologist. I didn't even ask her about the course of treatment or anything related to it. I trusted her completely. She made me feel comfortable, gave me confidence and reassurance. That is most important for a cancer patient and if an oncologist makes you feel that way, then they are the right fit for you. Here was an oncologist treating thousands of cancer patients each year, and if she said, I'll be fine then I knew I'll be fine. All I asked her at the time was, would the treatment hurt? Once again, Dr. Shanta smiled and replied, "Just a wee bit."

I was filled with happiness that fateful day and I am forever grateful to Dr. Shanta and the patients for inspiring me at the Cancer Institute. Hope brings with it so much positive energy and you start to feel good. The fear and anxiety you had may not melt away but it decreases. With hope, you can overcome challenges and obstacles. With hope, you start to get motivated. With hope, you gain the strength you need to face life.

My mantra to nurture hope:

1. Find the right oncologist.

2. Find inspiration.

3. Stay positive.

4. Seek emotional support.

5. Seek motivation.

6. Meditate.

7. Pray.

8. Seek therapy.

7

FAITH

Faith. Faith is what most of us turn to when we are going through tough times. And that is exactly what I did when I got to know about my breast cancer diagnosis. When one goes through a crisis, one holds on to faith because it gives one a sense of positivity, hope and a belief that things will ultimately turn out well. In 2004, I clung on to faith like never before. Faith had kept me going through the ups and downs in life and it was faith which was going to help me through this treatment and healing process.

When we talk about faith, we immediately associate it with religion. Not everyone follows a religion and faith doesn't necessarily mean religious belief – it also means having trust, belief and confidence. For me, however, faith meant having a religious belief which in turn gave me confidence that I will become well and life will be good.

I was born into a Hindu Tamil Brahmin family where religious customs and practices, along with daily prayers, were given utmost importance. My family loved visiting temples and took me along whenever they could. But they never imposed religion on me and my brother. Instead, they allowed us to practice our faith the way we chose to. Interestingly, I seem to have sub-consciously imbibed many of the aspects of my parents' religious practices over the years.

Once I began my treatment, my parents went on numerous trips to various temples across Tamil Nadu to pray for my health. I didn't have an opportunity to go with them because undergoing cancer treatment means you have to take a lot of precautions to protect your immunity and prevent infections. But my faith and belief in a higher power was unwavering and I prayed at home every day. I believed that I would get through the treatment and I would be hale and hearty once again but it would take time and there would be good and bad days. The treatment wasn't easy but faith in God got me through it.

You can be a believer or a non-believer. It doesn't matter. Just learn to trust - trust yourself, trust your doctors, and learn to feel strong and confident. That is what faith is ultimately about. Some of us turn to faith (meaning religion) only when we are going through a crisis. That's a personal choice, but I think we need to keep the faith going at all times, good and bad.

Going through cancer, life is uncertain and you are constantly plagued by self-doubt and questions – will you be fully cured? Will there be a remission later in life? Will you lead a normal life? Faith helps us believe that tomorrow will be better and as long as today goes well, it's a win.

Of the hundreds of books, I have read over the years, a quote from one particular one has been part of my life's motto since college.

In Margaret Mitchell's Gone With The Wind, Scarlett O'Hara says, "Tomorrow I'll think of some way… after all, tomorrow is another day".

As you may know, this quote is extremely popular. Though Scarlett is exhausted, she is extremely optimistic about the future and that she can deal with whatever comes her way tomorrow.

We need to have faith that tomorrow will be better. We need to have faith that we can handle anything that comes our way. Even though you may be going through treatment (or some crisis), you need to have faith that tomorrow will be better. You need to have faith that you are a strong person and you will get through it all, albeit slowly and steadily.

My mantra to develop faith:

1. Pray.

2. Meditate.

3. Read.

4. Believe.

5. Trust.

6. Journal.

7. Seek emotional support.

8. Practice gratitude.

POSITIVITY

Positivity. When people throw around the phrase 'be positive' in daily conversation, you don't think much of it. But when you have been diagnosed with cancer, you realise that 'be positive' becomes one of the most important phrases in your life. Right from the time of diagnosis, all you feel are negative emotions like fear, anger, anxiety, depression and hopelessness. Who can ever be positive about cancer? Is that even remotely possible?

Yes, it is possible, and you can and must be positive. When I first started chemotherapy and radiation, I was clueless about many things. A cancer patient would probably read books or articles on cancer or by cancer survivors. And me being a journalist, one would assume that would be the first step for me as well but no. The utter shock of the diagnosis in April 2004 got the better of me and I didn't look beyond the immediate steps of my treatment. However, there was a miraculous learning waiting to happen.

Bumbling along the first few weeks of treatment, I spent an exhausting amount of lamenting to friends and trying to be with them as much as possible. A routine had set in by the time my second chemo session was over – the first week of chemo was spent in bed at home, the second and third week meant I was out and about with friends, and doing medical tests, and then it was time for the next chemo. I started to count the 21 days to every chemo, then my surgery, recovery and so on.

Sitting at my friend's place one day after the second chemo, I was complaining yet again and she asked me, "How's your progress?"

"Good," I replied.

"What did Dr. Shanta tell you when you first met her?" she asked me.

"She said I'll be fine," I replied.

"Then why the hell are you complaining? She believes you'll be fine and you need to also," she replied.

And that's when the dark clouds in my mind parted and sun shone brightly. When my oncologist was positive, I needed to be positive. They knew better than me – they were doctors; they had studied medicine; this is what they practiced. What people – doctors, friends, and family – tell you, gives you positivity. Positive thinking is critical for your well-being (mental and physical) during cancer treatment and it gives you a fresh impetus for life. Consciously look for the sun between the dark clouds, find that silver lining and get your ducks in a row.

Organising consultant Marie Kondo, talks about picking up an object and asking, 'Does it spark joy?'. So, ask yourself what sparks joy and brings positivity to your life. Is it getting a pet? Is it painting? Is it going to the salon? Is it learning a new language? Is it planning a trip once your treatment is over?

My cancer treatment was a six-month process and after the second month, I started to truly live each day. I hardly spent time thinking about what would happen a few years down the line – I thought about now, tomorrow and the next few weeks. I needed to turn things around for myself, for my well-being.

Many women look at themselves in the mirror during treatment and feel sad about their appearance. Remember that this is a passing phase – your hair loss and weight loss are temporary. Don't mope about your looks. Look in the mirror and say this: I am beautiful; I am strong; I will get through this. Repeat these phrases several times a day and it will slowly boost your confidence. And yes, learn to look after yourself.

Self-care is critical as well during this period because it makes you feel good about yourself. So, what if you have a bald head or choose to wear a wig? So, what if you have lost weight and look thinner? It doesn't mean you can't dress up or wear make-up. It doesn't mean you can't go to dinner at a lovely restaurant. It doesn't mean you can't go the salon. It doesn't mean you can't go for walks on the beach or the park. It doesn't mean you can't watch a comedy and laugh your heart out.

Make sure you spend time on yourself and do what makes you feel nice. Make it a habit. This is a habit that will stand you in good stead for life as I have learnt.

When you are positive and feel good about yourself, then how others see you changes – they no longer look at you with sympathy, they look at you with awe.

My mantra to learn positivity:

1. Practice self-care.

2. Find joy.

3. Find inspiration.

4. Try new things.

5. Engage in activities.

6. Seek emotional support.

7. Seek therapy.

9

SELF-DISCOVERY AND LIFE

Self-discovery. Self-discovery is defined as 'the act or process of gaining knowledge or understanding of your abilities, character, and feelings'. This was a term I hardly paid credence to before my breast cancer diagnosis. Most people turn to self-discovery only when they cross 50 having lived most of their lives pursuing careers, looking after their families and raising their kids. And people often associate a mid-life crisis with self-discovery. This can't be further from the truth.

You don't need to have a mid-life crisis or hit 50 to go on a journey of self-discovery. It can happen at any point in your life, in any situation and at any age. At the age of 32, I wasn't into self-discovery (like a lot of other men and women) because I was focused on my career. However, the breast cancer diagnosis changed all that.

My life now is clearly divided into 2004 BC and 2004 AC – 2004 Before Cancer and 2004 After Cancer. I underwent a transformation – mentally and physically – and my personality changed as well. Before my cancer journey, I was more of an introvert, had lower self-esteem and was someone who looked at life as black and white. After my cancer journey, I became extremely outgoing, bold and had a devil-may-care attitude for most things in life. Social stigma, social mores and social acceptance be damned. This didn't mean I became a rebel and reckless – it just meant that I refused to let society dictate who I should be or not be and what I should do or not do.

My parents weren't conservative and they never restricted me from doing what I wanted. They had taught me to be a responsible adult and knew that I would never do anything that would cause them pain or grief. But society is not the same. People, especially in India, constantly judge you - your appearance, the way you behave, the way you dress, and so on. The question is – do you want to be you or do you want be something you are not?

Cancer changes you (not just physically but even emotionally) and I think every single cancer patient would concur. Many aspects of my personality took a 180 degree turn once I completed my treatment. Talking about a breast cancer diagnosis is not easy for many women because of the social stigma often attached in their community and so on. But I never hid it from anyone at any point in my life. For instance, I shaved my head because I wanted to be me. People could assume whatever they wanted about my bald head – I didn't owe anyone an explanation. On the other hand, some women opt to wear a wig because they are worried about social stigma. Others keep their head covered at all times. And I understand their situations too. As I said, what worked for me in some aspects may not work for all women but there were some fundamental lessons for all.

I spoke about my breast cancer journey openly, wrote about it in the media and gave breast cancer awareness talks as well. Public speaking was something I was terrified of 2004 BC but 2004 AC, I could get on any public platform and speak with ease on any subject as compared to my college days. This was a pleasant revelation for me.

As the years passed and I crossed every follow-up milestone with a negative diagnosis, my courage and strength went up in spades. I became more social and outgoing and started to look at life as 50 shades of gray rather than black and white. What was right for me could be wrong for someone else. And vice versa. But to each his own. I embraced everyone with their baggage and I wanted people to embrace me with mine. I wasn't perfect and I wasn't going to pretend I was. What people saw is what they got with me.

Post 2004, I made new friends, lost friends, joined numerous jobs, quit jobs, moved cities, travelled the world, lost Amma, lost Zen... the list is endless. But I discovered I had the courage and strength to get through it all successfully. And Amma stood by me stoically and provided constant encouragement till she moved on.

Losing Amma in 2019 was the second most painful incident in my life. She was diagnosed with breast cancer (Stage 3) in 2011 and Dr. Shanta was her oncologist as well. Now, I became her caregiver. The roles were reversed. I took care of her like how she had taken care of me and I wanted to ensure that I did the best or perhaps even more than the best. I just couldn't let her down. That was not an option. Unfortunately, she had a metastasis (brain tumor) and needed surgery in 2015. She smoothly crossed that as well but age-related complications resulted in her demise in November 2019 at the age of 76.

I thought I would be shattered when Amma passed away but I wasn't. I realized I was much stronger than what I gave myself credit for. I had organized her entire funeral and the 13-day Hindu religious rituals single-handedly shunning help from everyone. She was my Amma and I wanted to do everything for her by myself.

After her first death anniversary in 2020, I went to Varanasi and completed all the Hindu rituals one performs for the deceased for my Amma. My trip to Varanasi lasted 10 days and I went by myself. I wasn't afraid of going into the unknown but just nervous. Though I was exhausted after the trip, I knew she had been with me every step of the way. How else could I have performed the extensive rituals in Prayagraj, Varanasi and Gaya? How else could

I have travelled around with strangers? How else could I have courageously jumped into the deep Ganges?

My faith has grown stronger post my cancer recovery and I frequently visit temples across India. The belief that there is a higher power who gave us hope and strength to deal with life became more intense and I found peace and contentment.

Over the last decade, I have started to travel the world by myself. I have visited (and continue to visit) numerous countries solo and constantly try to engage in new experiences. For instance, I went tandem skydiving from 13000 feet in New Zealand. Imagine jumping out of a tiny airplane putting all your faith and trust in a stranger who has to get you to earth safely. Anything could go wrong – or not. It's a 50-50 chance. But I looked at the positive 50. I did it and I loved it. Now, I can't wait to do it again someday. After all, what is life without some adventure?

I could pen many more examples but I am sure you understand the fundamentals of self-discovery now. Everyone's journey of self-discovery is different and that's the beauty of life. Nature has ensured that no two human beings are alike which means that no two journeys on this earth are the same. Put the stamp on your journey your way.

My journey of self-discovery taught me this – figure out who you want to be in life; do what you think is right for you; do what makes you feel good; do what makes you happy; and find ways to enrich your life. Above all, be honest and sincere with your loved ones. They will be your biggest supporters and cheer you on.

Life will change post breast cancer and it's important to acknowledge and accept the change. Don't fight the change but find ways to accommodate it and make your life happier.

Remember - you are strong, beautiful and can conquer the world. Nothing can or will stop you but yourself.

This is just the beginning of a wonderful life. Now, go ride that pink elephant into the sunset.

ACKNOWLEDGEMENTS

My breast cancer journey started in 2004 and it has taken me 19 years to finally put it down on paper.

Thank you, Amma, Shanthi Srinivasan, for giving me the courage and resilience I desperately needed in life. Your words of wisdom ring in my ears constantly. You may no longer be here but I know you are watching over us.

Thank you, Appa, Srinivasan Pattoo, for all the things I learnt from you about life and for the passion for writing and travel you instilled in me.

Thank you, my bro, Ramkumar Srinivasan, for your advice and encouragement.

Thank you, Dr. V Shanta, for ensuring that I beat breast cancer, taking good care of me and holding my hand when I needed it the most.

Thank you, Vijaya, Harsh and Senthil Kumar for being my pillars of support during my breast cancer treatment.

Thank you to all my dear friends who stood by me through the ups and downs over the last two decades and for cheering me on.

Thank you, Notion Press, for believing in my book and helping me take it to the reader.

Last but not the least, thank you, dear readers. These words come to life only when you read them.

ABOUT THE AUTHOR

Latha Srinivasan is a senior journalist based in Chennai, India. The Pink Elephant is her debut book based on her breast cancer journey.

Latha is an award-winning journalist who has completed her M. Phil. in Sociology from the University of Madras. She was bestowed an Honorary Doctorate by Rai University in 2022 for her outstanding contribution in the field of Journalism and Health (Cancer Awareness).

She has worked with some of the best media organizations and is considered one of the leading entertainment journalists in South India.

A regular speaker and moderator at various national events, Latha does her share in society to increase awareness about breast cancer. She is an avid traveler who loves to experience different cultures and meet new people from around the world. Her motto in life is apt as well - change is the only constant.

Latha, who is very active on social media, currently lives in Chennai with her Appa and beloved Yuki.

Mail her: lathasrinivasan10@gmail.com

Tweet her: latasrinivasan